MICROSOFT WINDOWS 11 2023 GUIDE FOR BEGINNERS

SUOMAN AIRAGHT

INTRODUCTION

Welcome to the "Microsoft Windows 11 2023 Guide for Beginners", your comprehensive roadmap to exploring the multifaceted universe of Windows 11. It doesn't matter if you're a seasoned user of previous Windows versions or a newcomer to the world of personal computing; this guide is carefully tailored to meet the needs of every individual wanting to gain proficiency in using Windows 11.

Over the past few years, technological advances have reshaped the way we interact with machines, making the relationship between human and computer more symbiotic than ever. Microsoft, with its release of Windows 11, has acknowledged this evolution, introducing a plethora of new features, interface designs, and under-the-hood improvements that strive to enhance the user experience in unparalleled ways. As you delve deeper into this guide, you will find clear, step-by-step instructions to help you unlock the full potential of this revolutionary operating system.

Chapter 1 sets the stage by acquainting you with the essentials of Windows 11. You will be introduced to the new features and functionalities that set it apart from its predecessors. Did you know that the Start Menu has been relocated and is now more customizable than before? Or that there's an updated battery and HDR feature that can potentially revolutionize your multimedia experience? Ever wondered how your Android device could seamlessly interoperate with your Windows PC? All these and more will be unraveled in the initial chapter.

Moreover, Microsoft's continual efforts to enhance user experience through iterative feedback are evident with its Windows Insider Program. Dive deeper, and you'll understand the intricacies of the Beta Channel and the Channel for Release Preview, ensuring you're always at the forefront of Windows updates. Given the wave of change that Windows 11 brings, understanding its system requirements becomes imperative. The guide takes a deep dive into this, ensuring your transition is smooth, devoid of any hardware-software incompatibilities.

Navigating the vast landscape of Windows 11, as detailed in Chapter 2, is akin to being the captain of a technologically advanced spaceship. While the OS is designed to be intuitive, having a detailed guide will ensure you not only harness the primary features but truly master the advanced functionalities. Want to pin applications to the Start Menu? Or adjust sound settings like a pro? From changing password rules to installing Android applications, and even troubleshooting techniques using Task Manager, this chapter offers insights into the core workings of Windows 11.

The highlighted table of contents above is but a glimpse of the vast array of topics that this guide encompasses. As technology continues to evolve, so does the need for us to evolve with it. Windows 11, with its new design philosophy and advanced features, represents the future of personal computing. Yet, like every tool, its true potential can only be unlocked when wielded correctly.

This guide aims to be your companion in this journey of discovery. Whether you're a student aiming to maximize productivity, a professional looking to streamline workflows, or an enthusiast keen on exploring every nook and cranny of the new OS, there's something here for everyone. Embrace the future, demystify the complexities, and let the voyage of mastering Windows 11 begin!

So, fasten your seatbelts and get ready to dive into the intricate, exciting, and revolutionary world of Microsoft Windows 11. By the end of this guide, the hope is that you'll not only be proficient in navigating and using Windows 11 but also feel empowered to explore beyond, continually learning and adapting in our ever-evolving digital age.

While change can often be intimidating, especially when it comes to technological platforms we use daily, it's also an avenue of growth and innovation. Windows 11, in all its glory, represents Microsoft's vision for a digital future that is both accessible and advanced. The myriad of features introduced, from aesthetic revamps to performance improvements, emphasizes an ecosystem where user convenience is paramount. The shift isn't merely in terms of how the OS looks, but how it feels – a more tactile, intuitive, and user-friendly experience.

In our interconnected world, the boundaries between different operating systems and devices are blurring. This is evident in Windows 11's Android Device Interoperability feature, hinting at a future where your PC and mobile device don't just co-exist but synergize to enhance productivity and entertainment. Such an approach breaks down barriers, offering users more flexibility and options than ever before.

Chapter 1's foray into the nuances of Windows 11 is more than just an enumeration of features. It's an invitation. An invitation to explore, to experiment, and to experience. The relocation and customization of the Start Menu, the seamless Snap Layouts, the visually appealing Dark Mode, and the enhanced Microsoft Store, among others, are not just features – they are tools. Tools that allow you to tailor your computing environment to reflect your personal or professional needs.

As we move to Chapter 2, the guide shifts from the 'what' to the 'how'. It's one thing to know about the features and quite another to master their utilization. Detailed walkthroughs, from pinning applications to troubleshooting common issues, aim to empower even the most novice of users. After all, technology, in its truest essence, should be democratizing. It should be a platform where everyone, regardless of their prior knowledge or expertise, has an equal opportunity to learn, grow, and thrive.

But this guide is not just about the present. As you progress, you'll also gain insights into what the future might hold. With discussions around the Windows Insider Program and the ever-evolving landscape of updates, you'll be equipped to stay ahead of the curve, always ready to harness the latest that Windows has to offer.

In the forthcoming chapters, each topic, no matter how trivial it might seem, is treated with depth and clarity. This meticulous approach ensures that by the end of your journey through this guide, there will be no stone left unturned, no feature left unexplored.

In conclusion, Windows 11 isn't just an upgrade; it's a transformation. A transformation of how we perceive computing, how we interact with our devices, and how we envision the future of digital interaction. As you embark on this enlightening journey through the pages of this guide, remember that every innovation, every change, is an opportunity. An opportunity to learn, to adapt, and to be part of the next era of digital evolution.

Let's begin this adventure together, hand in hand, as we explore the vast, dynamic, and promising world of Microsoft Windows 11. Welcome aboard!

CONTENTS

Chapter 1: Basics of Windows 11 1

Microsoft Account and Internet Access 2

Windows 11 New Features..2

Relocating the Start Menu 2

Customization of the Start Menu 2

Use the Snap Layouts 2

Dark Mode 2

Android Device Interoperability...3

Efficient Windows Update Process..3

Configure Accessibility Options 3

Updated Battery 3

HDR 3

The New Microsoft Store 3

Windows 11 Will Be Available for Free!..4

Windows Insider Program..4

The Beta Channel..4

Channel for Release Preview 4

Windows 11 System Requirements 5

New Microsoft Store 6

New Microsoft Edge Features 7

New Features in the Calculator App 9

New Features in the Calendar and Mail App 10

New Features in Microsoft Teams 10

How to Install the Windows 11 Insider Preview 10

Getting the Windows 11 ISO File..14

Considerations Before Downloading Windows 11 Make Sure Your Computer Meets Windows 11 Requirements 14

Not All PCs that Run Windows 10 will Also Run Windows 11 15

How to Install and Download Windows 11 Using "Microsoft's Windows Download" Webpage 15

How to Use: 15

How to Install and Download Windows 11 Using the "Update and Security Feature" 16

How to Install Windows 11 on a PC 16

this device...21

Chapter 2: Navigating Windows 11..23

How to Pin Applications to the Start Menu 23

How to Arrange Pinned Applications 23

App Removal or Unpinning...24

Pinning Fresh Apps and Folders 25

How to Adjust the Sound Settings and Sound Volume 26

How to Set Up Security Settings for Windows 11..........................27

Making Use of a Password Manager...28

How to Change Password Rules for Microsoft Account 28

How to Customize Search Options..28

Installing Programs on Windows 11 30

How to Restore and Uninstall an Uninstallable Program.................31

How to Reduce the Size of a Partition in Windows 11.....................31

How...to

Increase the Size of a Partition in Windows 11 using Disk Management

....31

Delete Volume. 32

Extend Volume. 32

How to Create a Password for Your Microsoft Account...................32

How to Use A Task Manager to Troubleshoot................................32

How to Create Desktop Shortcuts 34

How to Check Drive Usage...35

How to Change the Name of Your Drive 35

How to Turn Off OneDrive 35

Determine Which Services you will Share with Microsoft................36

Installing Android Applications on Windows 11 36

How Do You Clone a Hard Drive to an SSD in Windows 11? 39

How to Repair Crashed Software in Windows 11 40

How to Change Your Keyboard Layout 41

How to Fix Bluetooth Using Troubleshooter 43

Troubleshoot. 43

How to Screenshot on Windows 11..44

How to Factory Reset on Windows 11...46

How to Switch Between Keyboards 48

How to Enable Touch Keyboard in Windows 11.............................48

How to Add Shortcuts to the Start Menu 49

How to Enable Clipboard History on Windows 11 50

How to Use Different Keyboard Layouts 51

How to Configure Keyboard Layouts in Windows 11 51

How to Modify the Keyboard Layout in Windows 11 51

Taskbar. 52

How to Remove Keyboard Layout in Windows 11 52

Emoji Keyboard in Windows 11 52

How to Use Windows 11 Emoji Keyboard 53

Use the Shortcut (Windows +; full stop) or (Windows 53

Use the Windows 11 On-screen Keyboard to Access the Emoji

Keyboard 53

How to Access the Command Prompt in Windows 11 53

How to Go Back to Windows 10 55

Insider. 56

How to Use the Transparency Effect in Windows 11 57

How to Disable Windows 11 Transparency Effects.......................58

How to Open Your File Explorer in Windows 11 59

Access Your File Explorer from the Taskbar 60

Select it from the Start Menu 60

Launch ....File

Explorer by Searching for and Opening It 60

Using a Shortcut Keyboard...60

Run Commands to Open Your File Explorer 60

How to Enable Classic Ribbon Menu in File Explorer 61

How..Do

You Change from Standard User to Administrator in Windows 11?62

Navigate to Settings and Select Administrator 62

Switch to Administrator Mode Using the Control Panel...................63

Change the Administrator Making Use of Command Prompt..........65

Windows 11's Quick Settings...65

Adding or Deleting 66

Removing Quick Settings 66

Using Windows 11 to Connect to a Wi-Fi Network.........................66

Automatic Reconnect...67

Installing Fonts on Windows 11 67

How to Change the Primary Monitor in Windows 11 69

How Can I Change the Primary Monitor? 69

Fill in Your Preferences or Settings 69

Display Option 70

The Monitor Menu..70

How to Take a Screenshot in Windows 11 71

How Do I Take a Screenshot in Windows 11? 71

Snipping Instrument...71

Sketch & Snip 71

How to Reset Windows 11 To Factory Settings 72

Refresh Your Computer..72

Reboot Your Computer...73

Reset the System 73

Install Everything from the Start...74

Windows 10 to Windows 11 Upgrade..74

Is the Upgrade from Windows 10 to Windows 11 Free? 74

Is Windows 11 Suitable for My Computer? 75

How Can You Tell If Your Computer is Ready for Windows 11? 75

Windows 11 VPN Configuration 75

Address Box. 76

Best VPN to Use on Windows 11 76

Newly Added Shortcuts in Windows 11 77

Conclusion 78

Chapter 1: Basics of Windows 11

The Best Tools for Windows 11

Microsoft Visual Studio is a desktop, server, and mobile development environment that aims to provide a consistent user experience across devices. Visual Studio 15.2 introduces new Windows app development tools that speed up app development. Users can create apps for Windows 11, iPhone, and Android using the Visual Studio Technical Preview for Python. It supports the addition of a one-time code execution environment in the cloud. In addition, Visual Studio 15.2 improves the developer experience in NET development.

It has some interesting new features, such as the ability to download and run Android applications, attractive designs, good and improved security, better PC gaming experiences, ease of use, and creativity. Unlike previous versions of Windows, which required installing system software locally on your computer, Windows 11 allows you to store all key components in the cloud.

However, Microsoft will notify all users when the update becomes available in the coming months. To Microsoft's credit, the Windows team has done an excellent job developing this operating system, which no longer has the flaws of the previous Windows operating system.

Microsoft Account and Internet Access

Moving out of Windows 11 Home in S-mode necessitates internet use, and all Windows 11 versions require Internet access to perform upgrades, install, and use some features. Certain features will also require the use of a Microsoft account.

Certain functions necessitate the use of hardware as well. Some applications will have higher system requirements than Windows 11's minimum requirements, so you can check the compliance information for the applications you want to install. The amount of storage on your computer varies according to the programs and upgrades you have installed. The performance will improve as personal computers become more powerful. As time passes and more changes are made, additional criteria may become necessary.

Windows 11 New Features

You can personalize your recently upgraded system by right-clicking on the **Windows** icon on the desktop and selecting **Settings**. This includes everything from relocating the **Start** button to checking the configuration of external monitors.

Relocating the Start Menu

The **Start** button (along with all of the shortcuts you previously pinned) is now located on your PC's Taskbar, one of the most noticeable differences between Windows 11 and previous versions of Windows.

Customization of the Start Menu

By heading to the **Settings** area and choosing **Personalization** and the **Start** option, you determine whether or not to show newly launched items and specific directories on the **Start** menu. When you press the **Start** key, you'll be presented with options and toggle switches to help you decide what to see.

Use the Snap Layouts

While Windows 10 allows you to 'dock' apps on half of the screen by dragging them to the sides, Windows 11 gives you more layout options.

Dark Mode

Almost all software on the market now includes a dark mode feature. You can switch to this mode from **Settings** by going to **Personalization>Colors** and then choosing the desired mode from the dropdown menu.

Android Device Interoperability

The **Your Phone** feature in Windows 11 improves on the previous version. This simplifies connecting your Android smartphone to your laptop, allowing you to transfer files between machines and send SMS from your PC.

Efficient Windows Update Process

Microsoft improved the process of updating your system in Windows 11 so that you can view (and control) some of these innovative features by going to Settings and selecting Windows Update.

Configure Accessibility Options

The Ease of Access menu has been renamed the Accessibility menu in Windows 11, making the current edition of Microsoft's operating system more accessible. The options are closed captions, eye control, color filters, and font size.

Updated Battery

Windows 11's battery health panel has been updated and improved. To find it, navigate to **Settings>System>Power & Battery**. There is a more in-depth examination of how battery capacity changes over time and what causes power drain. Scroll down to **Battery Usage** to see which programs have used the most power from your PC since you plugged it in.

HDR

High Dynamic Range, also called HDR, balances the brightest and darkest portions of the contents on your PC's display, ensuring that all elements are visible. The functionality was featured in Windows 10, but Windows 11 offers additional gaming support.

The New Microsoft Store

This part will walk you through finding and installing the best applications, games, videos, and even great deals, such as exclusive discounts for Xbox Game Pass subscribers. The content on the Microsoft Store has been thoroughly vetted for device compatibility, family safety, and security. Microsoft gave select application developers a sneak peek at their projects and a slew of great apps, including Disney+, Adobe Creative Cloud, Zoom, TikTok, and a few of its programs like Visual Studio, Microsoft Teams, and even Paint and Notepad, which will be available in the new Microsoft Store on Windows 11.

The Microsoft Store was rebuilt from the ground up, providing more content while maintaining a responsive and simple customer experience. Here's a sneak peek at some of Windows 11's most compelling features:

- Popular applications and videogames with curated collections and stories.

- Compatible with android games and applications.

- Amazon applications UI.

- A more developer-friendly Microsoft Store – compliant with a broader range of applications.

Windows 11 Will Be Available for Free!

One of the most common questions potential Windows 11 users present is whether they will have to pay to use it. Windows 11 is a free upgrade for anyone who has already installed Windows 10. So, whether your computer is technically enabled or not, if you are running Windows 10 Pro or Home, you can install and activate Windows 11.

Windows Insider Program

The tech giant announced the impending release of Windows 11 in June 2021 and is currently providing preview versions to select Windows Insider program participants. On October 5, 2021, the new operating system went live. The Windows Insider program is divided into three channels: **development**, **testing**, and **production**.

New features are released in the Dev Channel for preliminary testing, regardless of which Windows version they will eventually appear in. This channel is best suited for technical users and developers, but installations can be unpredictable and problematic.

The Beta Channel

This channel contains more advanced capabilities that will be included in the next major Windows release. The Beta Channel is ideal for beta testers, and Microsoft claims that your feedback will have the most impact here.

Channel for Release Preview

The Release Preview Channel is typically not used until just before the release of new feature updates. It's ideal for people who want the most dependable variants and is intended for final testing of a future rollout.

The Beta Channel receives previews for the early release of Windows 11, whereas the Dev Channel evaluates potential inclusions for Windows 11 upgrades following the initial October 5th rollout. Corporate computers in the Release Preview Channel received the corporate preview of Windows 11 on September 9, 2021.

Not everyone will be qualified to join the Windows 11 Insider program because the new operating system has more strict requirements than its predecessor. According to a Microsoft article, if your computer does not meet the minimum system requirements for Windows 11, you will be unable to join the Beta or Dev Channels. Instead, you will join the Release Preview Channel to test Windows 10 preview upgrades.

If you are already a Dev Channel Windows 10 Insider member and your computer does not meet the system requirements, you may still receive Windows 11 previews for the time being. Computers that do not meet the minimum requirements will not receive Windows 11 Insider Preview builds until Windows 11 is broadly released.

Windows 11 System Requirements

Windows 11 will be compatible with systems that can run the Windows 10 system software. In addition, current Windows 10 users can download the Windows 11 operating system for free. Regarding software testing, you should be cautious about installing the beta version of the system software on your primary device because it may contain unresolved bugs. Microsoft is clear that most Windows PCs will be able to run the new Windows 11, but the system requirements for the New Windows 11 operating system are as follows:

- **Processor:** 1 GHz or faster with two or more cores on a compatible 64-bit processor or system on a chip RAM: 4GB

- **Storage:** 64GB or greater System firmware: UEFI with Secure Boot capability

- **TPM:** Trusted Platform Module (TPM) Version 2.0 Display: HD (720p) display greater than 9 inches diagonally, 8 bits per color channel Graphics Card: Compatible with DirectX 12 or later with WDDM 2.0 driver

- **Internet Connection and Microsoft account:** An Internet connection and a Microsoft account will be needed for the device setup and updates.

To use the new Windows 11, the system specification in the screenshot below must be met:

- A modern 1Ghz 64-bit dual-core processor
- 4GB RAM
- 64GB drive
- 9-inch display

- 1366x768 resolution
- UEFI, Secure Boot & TPM 2.0 compatible
- DirectX 12 compatible graphics / WWDM 2.x

There are drawbacks to these system specifications, as most people have one or two reservations about them. One of the disadvantages for the Windows community is that the Windows 11 operating system will only be accessible on computers with 64-bit architecture. The Windows 11 operating system does not have a 32-bit version, but do not be concerned. If you have 32-bit applications, they will continue to function correctly under the new operating system.

In addition, Microsoft is not ready to release the official Windows 11 to users older than the Intel 8th generation. This means that if your computer has a CPU older than the Intel 8th generation, you will not be able to launch Windows 11 operating system comfortably. However, Microsoft made an exception to the Intel 7th-generation and the AMD Ryzen 1000 series CPUs, adding that they can run the Windows 11 operating system easily.

The new Windows 11 also needs a display size of at least 9-inches. This means that your mini 8-inch tablets or phones will be unable to run Windows 11 due to limiting screen size. In addition, Microsoft has increased the minimum drive storage to about 64GB, up from the former 16GB with Windows 10. RAM was not left out, as it has been raised from 2GB to 4GB.

New Microsoft Store

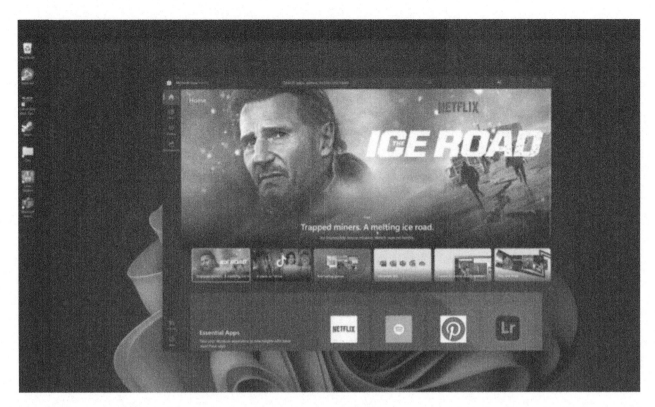

Windows 11 now includes a new Microsoft Store. One fantastic new feature of this Microsoft store is the ability to install and use Android apps on your Windows device.

These Android apps are available for download from the Amazon store, which has been integrated into the Microsoft store. To use this feature, go to the **Taskbar** and click on the **Microsoft Store**. From the Microsoft store home page, go to the **Amazon Store** for a list of Android apps.

Choose an app and then install it. To use the Amazon store, you must first create an Amazon account. The gaming feature in Windows 11 now includes an X Box game pass and auto HDR. This new feature will improve your gaming experience by enhancing your games.

New Microsoft Edge Features

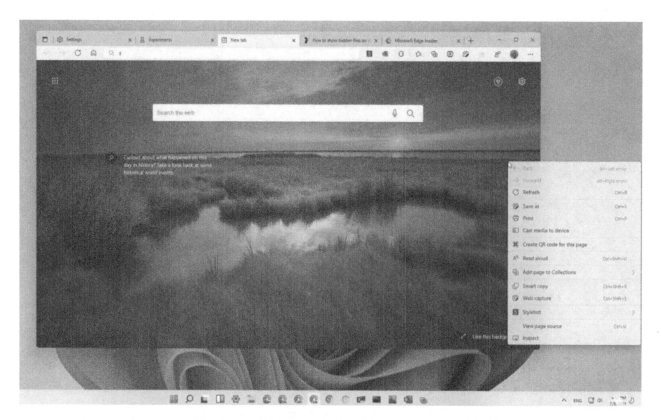

Microsoft Edge 93 gets new features in Windows 11. The browser's overall appearance has been updated as the menu elements in the new Microsoft Edge are semi-transparent. This means you can see a small portion of the content at the bottom of the menu. The increased glass-like appearance of the Microsoft edge now blends seamlessly with the Windows 11 dark theme.

These visual elements may not be enabled by default, so you must enable them manually via advanced settings. This feature may become readily available with the official release of Windows 11.

1. First, ensure that the most recent edition of Microsoft Edge is installed on your Windows 11. Go to the **Microsoft Edge Insider Page** and select the **Canary Channel** if you don't already have it. Accept and download by clicking **Accept**.

2. Launch the new **Microsoft Edge Canary Browser** after it has been downloaded.

3. You can search for updates if you already have Microsoft Edge installed on your computer. Go to your browser's settings to accomplish this. Click the options icon **(...)** from your browser page and then **Settings**.

4. Scroll down to the bottom of the left menu and select **About Microsoft Edge**. Microsoft Edge will start looking for updates. You

can proceed to the next step if your Microsoft Edge browser is up to date.

5. Open a new tab in the new **Microsoft Edge Canary Browser** and enter **edge:/flag**. This will take you to the Windows experiment page.

6. Enter **Windows 11 Visual Updates** in the search field. You will see an option that is similar to your search keywords. Click the **Default Dropdown** button on the right side of the option.

7. Choose **Enabled**.

8. To apply the changes, click **Restart** in the bottom right corner. The new visual changes will be applied to your Microsoft Edge browser.

New Features in the Calculator App

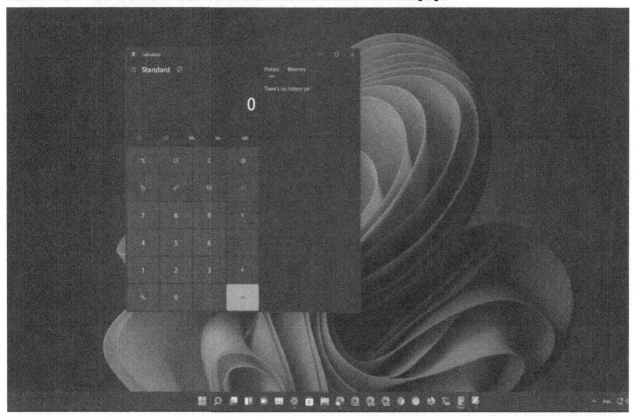

The latest update of Windows 11 brings new features to the calculator app. More elements and a new design with rounded corners have been introduced. According to Microsoft, the scientific and programmer calculator has now been improved.

In addition, the currency feature in the calculator can now be used to convert up to 100 different currency units.

New Features in the Calendar and Mail App

The calendar app also features a few changes but remains the same as in Windows 10 except for the new rounded corners and some little icon changes.

There have also been some little changes in the mail app to match with Windows 11, although it still looks the same as the mail app in Windows 10. One of the noticeable visual changes is the rounded edges of the App.

New Features in Microsoft Teams

With the new Microsoft teams chat updates, Microsoft has taken its competitors head-on as it now offers more than text chats. You can now make video and audio calls using Microsoft Teams in Windows 11. You can now create meetings and even join one utilizing this App.

It also offers tools to help you disable your camera or microphone if you want some privacy. To make it more interesting, you can now share your screen to allow friends to join the chat.

When you click open **Microsoft Teams** at the bottom of the page, you'll be directed to a page where you can manage your chat settings. Here you can see the list of participants and adjust the conversation.

How to Install the Windows 11 Insider Preview

Windows 11 is now available and includes some excellent features that you may appreciate. Users can now look at the new features added to the previous version of Windows 10. Because it may seem unfamiliar with these new features, we have reviewed what to expect in the latest Windows 11 as it would be unwise to dive in immediately. For the reasons stated above, Microsoft developers created an Insider Preview, as this will show you what the most recent update is all about.

As a result, we'll look at how to install the new Windows 11 insider preview.

1. Before downloading the Windows Insider raw file and installing it on your PC, ensure that your PC is secure and that your data cannot be compromised.

2. You must then determine whether your system meets the requirements for Windows 11 as outlined above.

3. Following that, you back up your system files to an external hard drive or any other storage device, including an external cloud server. It's fine to look at the latest Windows preview, but it isn't good if you do so at the expense of your personal files. After safely backing up your files, you can begin the installation.

4. To get Windows 11 right away, you must be a member of Microsoft's insider program, which you can sign up for on their website. On the other hand, you can join the insider program in Windows 10 by going to the Start Menu and selecting Insider.

5. Proceed and click **Settings**.

6. Next, select **Update and Security**.

7. Then click on the **Windows Insider Program** from the left side of the menu. You need to send Microsoft your diagnostic data before getting the Windows 11 preview builds. The system will prompt you to make that decision because you won't proceed until you enable "Optional Diagnostic Data" in the Diagnostic data panel in the **Settings** menu.

8. You do not need to track down the process as long as you enable it. Microsoft will prompt you to link to the **Diagnostic & Feedback** menu.

9. Once that has been concluded, you can proceed to link the accounts directly. Click **link an account** and select the account to link.

10. *Next, proceed and select Dev Channel and then click* *on* **Confirm.**

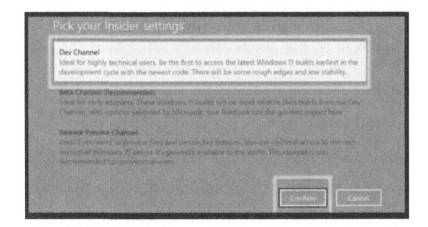

11. Follow the prompts that appear after and then proceed to get Windows 11.

12. You will be asked to preview the Microsoft Insider Policy Agreement carefully. Once you're done with that, you click on the **Confirm** button.

13. Next, click on **Restart** to reboot your PC and get access to the Windows 11 Insider Preview to build.

14. Once your system has finished booting, you need to connect your PC to an internet connection, proceed to Settings, choose Update & Security, and click **Check for Updates**.

15. The PC will then start downloading the latest build from the Microsoft cloud.

Getting the Windows 11 ISO File

First and foremost, you must have a Windows 11 ISO file. They are disk images that can be used to create bootable External Storage, allowing you to install any version of Windows from a USB flash drive or an optical CD. Because Microsoft does not provide ISO files, you must obtain them from a third-party website called uupdump.net.

1. Go to **uupdump.net.**

2. Click on the **x64 icon** for the most recent Dev Channel build.

3. Afterward, select the most recent build, proceed, and click **Next**.

4. Select the Windows edition you require, then click **Next**. For the Windows 11 ISO, Windows Home is the better option.

5. Select **download and convert to ISO** and **Create Download Package**. Your computer will receive a zip file.

6. Unzip the uup file's contents and save them in a secure location.

7. Double-click the download **windows.cmd** in the folder containing your downloaded files.

8. Select **Run Anyway**. A command prompt will appear, with a batch file running that displays the details of the file you're downloading from Microsoft.

9. Depending on your internet speed, this may take some time to complete.

Considerations Before Downloading Windows 11
<u>Make Sure Your Computer Meets Windows 11 Requirements</u>

If your PC meets the requirements, you must back up your files before proceeding. This helps save your files if something goes wrong during the upgrade process, as upgrading to a new operating system is dangerous.

Not All PCs that Run Windows 10 will Also Run Windows 11

If you have Windows 7 (or any later version), you will receive a free upgrade to Windows 11. You may be in a hurry to download it, but it is best to wait, especially if you only have one PC. Because it is a major operating system, there will almost certainly be early issues.

How to Install and Download Windows 11 Using "Microsoft's Windows Download" Webpage

1. Your PC must be compatible with the Windows 11 upgrade requirements.

2. Go to **www.microsoft.com**. On this website, you will have three options for installing and upgrading Windows 11.

3. The first option is **Windows 11 Installation Assistant**, which uses an assistant. This is the easiest part of installing Windows 11, but your PC must have at least 10GB of free disk space for Windows 11 to be able to download

How to Use:

1. Download the **Installation Assistant**. Click **Run**. To be able to run this, you must be an administrator

2. The tool will confirm if the device is compatible. If it is, a pop-up menu will show you the license terms. Click **Accept and Install**.

3. After installation, click on the **Restart Now** button to complete your installation. Do not turn off your PC.

How to Install and Download Windows 11 Using the "Update and Security Feature"

1. Back up your files on an external drive or the cloud.

2. On your PC, tap on the **Start** icon, and go to **settings**.

3. *Click on **Update and Security** and tap on the windows update inside the program option.*

4. *Click on **Check for Updates**. If your PC is compatible, the Windows 11 update will be made available for you.*

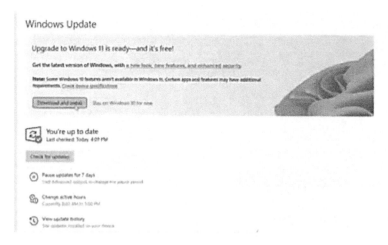

5. After making it available to you, click **Download and Install.**

6. You are to restart your PC for the installation process and configure the settings.

How to Install Windows 11 on a PC

I recommend creating a new partition if you wish to use the old Windows 10 version. Else you can format the old windows and install them as a new OS.

1. To install Windows 11, you have first to boot the PC you want to install it on using the USB installation storage. Make a boot order beforehand so that it will boot accordingly.

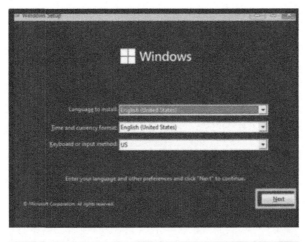

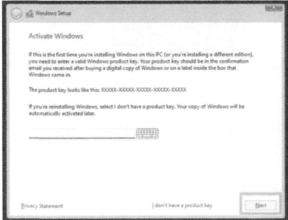

2. Next, select the language you prefer for the windows and click **Next**.

3. Enter a **Product Key** or choose **"I don't have a product key."** Proceed and tap **Next**.

4. Tick on the box provided to accept the License and Agreement. Then click **Next**.

5. Choose **Custom Install**. Click **Next** after.

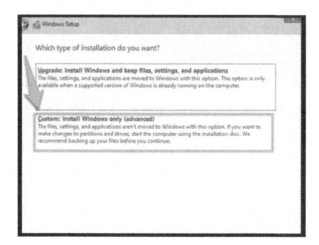

6. Next, select the preferred drive for installation and tap **Next**.

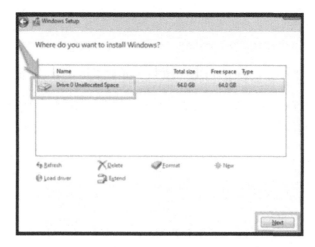

7. The Installer will proceed and copy some files, which may take a while. It may reboot after some time in the process.

8. The next step is to choose your country/region and tap **Yes**. Additionally, choose the keyboard layout when it's time for it.

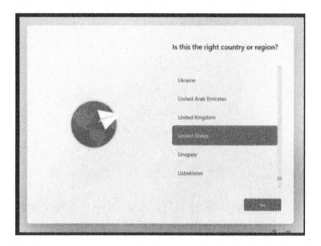

9. Input the name for your PC and tap **Next.**

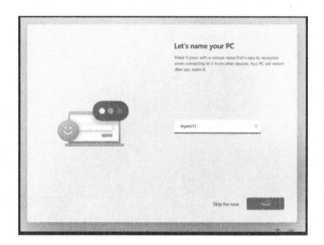

10. Next, sign in with your Microsoft account.

11. Create a PIN for when you want to log in quickly.

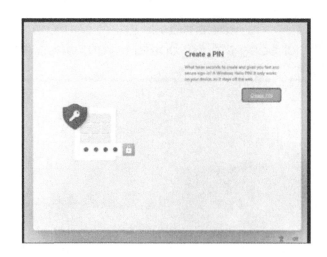

12. Tap **Set Up as New Device** unless you want to restore a previous configuration.

13. Tick or untick privacy settings and click **Next.**

14. Choose the features that you like when customizing your

Windows 11, or you can skip this process.

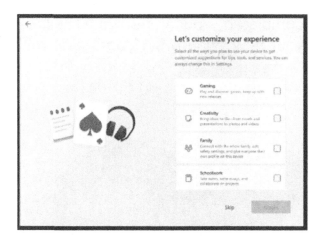

15. Package **OneDrive** or choose **Only Store Files on this device.**

16. Windows will take a few moments to finish the installation process.

Once this has been completed, your Windows 11 will be displayed for you to see. You can browse your new Windows 11 and even make some stings to suit the way you work.

Chapter 2: Navigating Windows 11

Start Menu and Storage

The first noticeable thing in the Windows 11 system update is the Taskbar, centered at the bottom of the display. According to the CEO of Microsoft, this is meant to center the whole Windows experience on its users.

How to Pin Applications to the Start Menu

Pinned apps help speed up your operation. To pin applications to the start menu, follow the steps below:

1. To pin apps in the start menu, go to the **Start** menu by clicking on the **Windows** icon.

2. To see a list of all your apps, click **All Apps**.

3. Right-click any app and select **Pin** to start.

How to Arrange Pinned Applications

Follow these methods for organizing pinned apps:

1. To add an application to the Taskbar, right-click it and select **Pin to Taskbar**.

2. Squeeze and hold (or right-click) a program to access **More > Pin to Taskbar**.

3. If the program is already open in the work area, choose **Pin to Taskbar** by squeezing and holding (or right-tapping) the taskbar button.

4. To remove an application from the Taskbar, go to the program's **Jump List** and select **Unpin from the Toolbar**.

App Removal or Unpinning

Some apps are inactive and should not be kept in the Start menu. You can delete these apps to make room for others you use frequently.

1. To accomplish this, tap on the **Windows** icon to open the **Start** menu.

2. Right-click the app you want to unpin or remove from the Start menu.

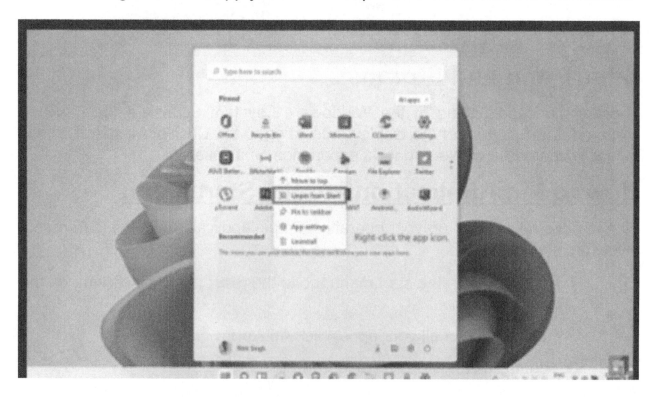

3. Tap on **Unpin from Start,** and it's done immediately.

Pinning Fresh Apps and Folders

You have the liberty to put all your valuable applications and folders in the Start menu so you can reach them anytime you desire. The process to do that is listed below:

1. Tap on the **Windows** icon to open the **Start** menu.

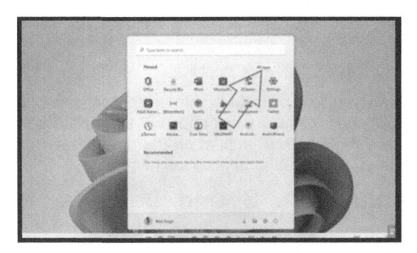

2. A list of all applications and programs on the system will be displayed. Navigate to the particular App you want to add to the **Start** Menu.

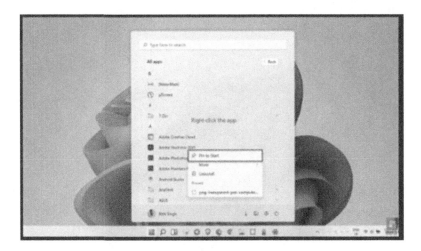

3. Right-click on the chosen application and then click **Pin to Start.**

4. To put additional folders on the **Start** menu, click on the **File Explorer** icon to open it. Next, proceed to the desired folder, right-click on it, and choose **Pin to Start.**

Windows 11 allows you to pin up to eighteen applications/folders to the Start menu. When it's finished, pinning more apps will trigger the creation of another page. Moving down the menu or tapping on the dotted navigation on the right-hand side will take you to the other application pages.

How to Adjust the Sound Settings and Sound Volume

This function has become more complicated in this version of Windows for some reason. Previously, you would go to the far right corner of your windows and change the sound. But now, when you click on the sound and volume icon, it takes you to the action center.

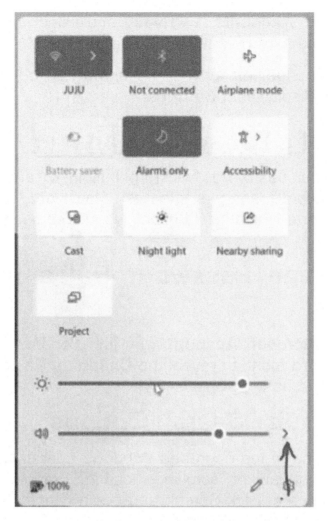

Sound is one of the options in the action center. You can change which speakers to use by clicking on the small arrow on the far right. In terms of sound, you can make additional adjustments. You can also access the settings by searching for sound settings in the search bar.

Another way to access your sound settings is to move your mouse to the sound icon and right-click. Choose between opening the volume mixer and the sound settings. The main difference is that it controls the sound from there via the action center when you click on it.

How to Set Up Security Settings for Windows 11

Setting up Windows 11 and mobile devices to lock down your security settings is simple, but you must first access your settings.

1. To access the **Microsoft Account** section, go to **My Microsoft Account** and **Settings & Privacy**.

2. Then, go to **Accounts & Privacy** and select the **Security** tab. You will then see a list of features and sections.

3. Select the page with privacy options at the bottom of the **Security** section to display your **Settings**.

Making Use of a Password Manager

You can manage your passwords with the built-in or a third-party password manager app. Password managers such as 1Password, Dashlane, LastPass, Keeper, and RoboForm are available, but we recommend using an account manager.

How to Change Password Rules for Microsoft Account

Find your selected **Microsoft Account** from the dropdown menu on the page and click the **Password** menu to reveal the **Changing Password** section. Click the **Change Password** button.

How to Customize Search Options

Windows search is one of the upgraded Windows operating system's cool and powerful features. Instead of scrolling, locating various applications, and identifying where they are, click Search and begin typing for the App. This will look for Apps as well as all other components on the computer. It will look for documents, websites, people, photos, videos, etc.

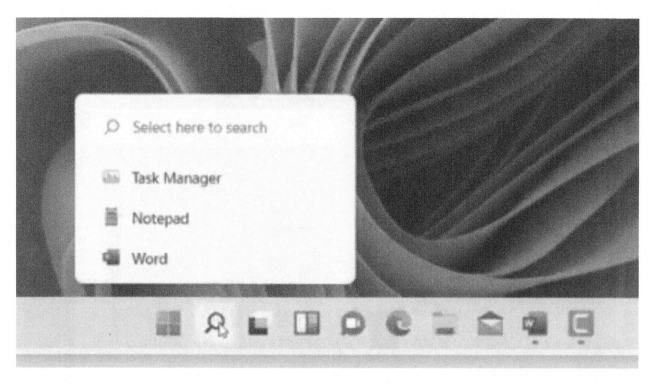

The search options can be customized by clicking on the three dots or options icon on the far right. You can also customize various icons and customize their search settings as well.

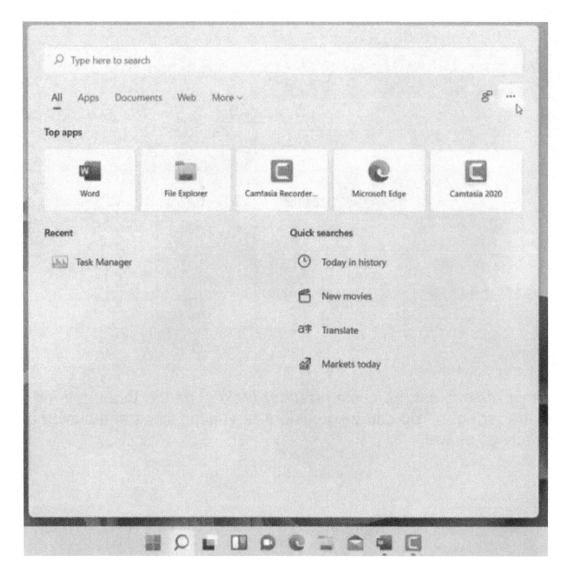

Start a search by clicking the **Windows** icon, pressing the Windows key, and typing. So, you can type the application's name into the search bar, click on it, and it will bring it up. You can also look for **Settings** on your computer. When it appears, you can modify the display settings by navigating to the display area or any display component and adjusting various settings such as scaling.

Installing Programs on Windows 11

If you previously installed Windows programs, they will still be present. If you reinstall a program from the Windows Store, the new version will replace the old one.

Instead of installing programs in batches, you must do so individually. Here's how to download and install programs in Windows 11.

1. To begin, navigate your **Documents** folder and locate the **Programs and Features** folder. This folder will hold all your downloaded files,

such as programs purchased from the Windows store or installed programs. If you haven't installed any programs in the past, they won't appear in this folder because they haven't been installed; similarly, if you have any programs installed on your Windows, they won't appear in this folder.

2. Once you've located your **Programs and Features** folder, you can download the most recent version of the program you'd like to install.

A large number of programs are now free to download. If you previously purchased a program, you could similarly download and install the most recent version of that program.

After purchasing a program on Windows 10, you may discover that you must pay for it, but this does not appear to be the case on Windows 11. Only programs that require your credit card information will require payment.

You can install Windows updates and individual applications with a single click if you have Windows 11 Professional or Enterprise.

How to Restore and Uninstall an Uninstallable Program

You might want to uninstall an uninstallable application now and then. The key found in the **About** window is the most straightforward way to accomplish this.

First, press the Delete key to remove a program, then select **Delete from the Start Menu**. Right-click on it, and then choose **Remove**.

How to Reduce the Size of a Partition in Windows 11

1. Right-click the **Windows** logo in the Taskbar.

2. Select **Disk Management**.

3. Right-click on **the NTFS Partition** and select **Shrink Volume**.

4. Enter the amount of space you want to shrink. (Note: 1024MB=1GB; if no amount is entered, the maximum available free space is used by default.)

How to Increase the Size of a Partition in Windows 11 using Disk Management

1. Right-click the correct adjacent partition (for example, D:) and select **Delete Volume.**

2. Right-click the left adjacent partition (for example, C:) and select **Extend Volume.**

3. Several clicks are required to complete the **Extend Volume Wizard** pop-up.

4. To make a Windows 11 partition larger, Extend Volume by right-clicking the partition you want to extend and selecting **Extend Volume** (this partition must have unassigned space immediately after it). Then, fine-tune a size for the amount of space you require. By default, the value is fixed to the absolute max permitted.

How to Create a Password for Your Microsoft Account

While a password manager like Dashlane can help, you should also consider how you'll share your account information with others.

The simplest way to share your Microsoft Account with others is to use your own Microsoft account. This gives them access to your Microsoft account from any computer or device equipped with a browser.

Dashlane's software includes this option, so the password manager automatically signs you in when you log in to your Microsoft Account. However, it implies that everyone in your family can access your account information and passwords. Of course, you can limit who has access to your Microsoft Account by configuring a **Master Password**.

How to Use A Task Manager to Troubleshoot

Previously, task managers were part of the Taskbar. So, when you right-click on the Taskbar, you'll see a task manager option. That, however, is no longer available. A task manager can be found by searching the start menu or Windows search.

There are a few other ways to reach the task manager.

If you right-click on the **Start** menu, there is also the option to click on **Task Manager**, and it will take you typically to the task manager for the first time unless you change it. So, it will list the applications that are running on your computer. However, if you want additional details like what's running in the system and the processing that is taking place, and so on, then click on more details, and you'll see the processes currently running on the PC.

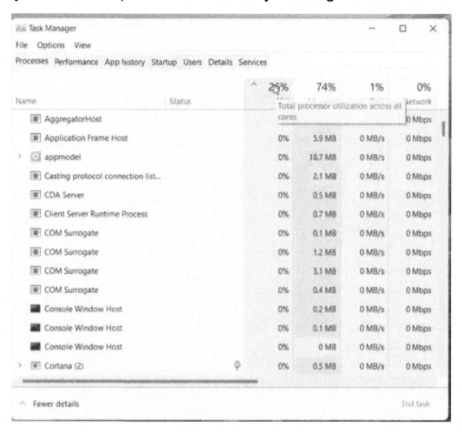

If the PC is running, the fans are running loud, there is typically an issue with the PC, or there is one of the applications in the computer that you need to stop. To identify which application is causing that issue, scroll up to the CPU and click the CPU utilization %. You can sort the files from highest to lowest.

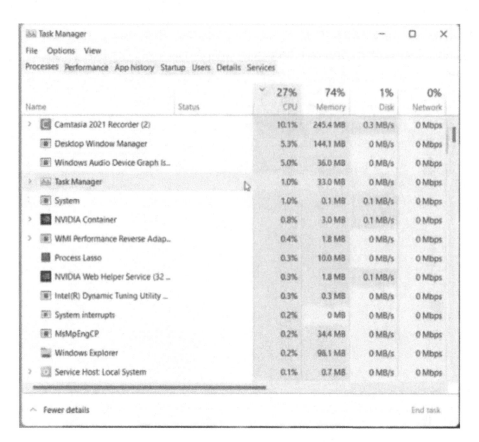

So, if there is something that you need to close, click on it and then click on **End Task**, which will close the process. It is not always the CPU that is slowing down your system. Certain apps may be consuming the majority of the memory. So, you can do the same thing with memory to determine what is using most of your computer's memory.

When the disk is struggling, you can tell you have a problem with the speed of your disk. You can also see how the processor or different components perform over time. So, if you click on CPU, you'll see the usage under memory usage, solid-state drives, wireless drives, graphics card, and so on.

How to Create Desktop Shortcuts

1. By pressing and holding (or right-clicking) the desktop, select **New > Shortcut**.

2. In **File Explorer**, type the item's location or select **Browse** to find it.

3. To remove a shortcut from your desktop, press and hold (or right-click) it, then select **Delete**.

4. When you delete a shortcut, you only remove the shortcut, not the actual object. (Note: You will not be able to create shortcuts for Windows Store applications.)

How to Check Drive Usage

Simply follow the steps below to view your drive's usage:

1. Navigate to the **Settings** tab.

2. Select the **Manage Disks and Volumes** option.

3. To view it, click on the **Properties** button.

4. Scroll down to the **View Usage** section of the settings page.

This is where you can see a list of the folders on the device and the amount of space they take up. You can view the contents and sizes of any folder by clicking on it.

How to Change the Name of Your Drive

Windows automatically tags drives with alphabets that distinguish them. Any drive, disc, or other media stored in a system has a name up to 32 (NFTS) or 11 (FAT) characters long. Users can also give their drives unique names to improve the user experience.

All drives in a PC are typically given a drive name, which allows users to identify them quickly. There are no limitations to the name you can give your drive because it is entirely up to you. You must be logged in as an administrator to change the drive's label. To successfully rename a drive in Windows 11, follow these steps:

1. Locate this PC in **Windows Explorer**.

2. Right-click on the drive and select **Properties**.

3. Another option is to press both **Win+X** and then select **Disk Management**.

4. Hold the **Shift** key while right-clicking on the drive you want to rename. Properties can also be accessed by tapping on them.

5. The name of the drive can be found in the **General** tab. Change the old name and replace it with the preferred name.

6. Click **OK** after selecting **Apply**.

How to Turn Off OneDrive

Go to your **Microsoft Account** page and select **Settings**, then **Cloud** settings. Under cloud services, select **Manage Privacy** and then select the button for your **OneDrive** account. To delete your OneDrive account, click the **Remove** button.

Determine Which Services you will Share with Microsoft

1. When using a password manager like Dashlane, you should think about how you'll share your account information with others.

2. Using your own Microsoft account is the simplest way to share your Microsoft Account with others. This allows them to access your Microsoft account from any computer or device that has a browser.

Dashlane's software includes this option so that when you log in to your Microsoft Account, the password manager automatically signs you in. However, it implies that everyone in your family can access your account information and passwords. Of course, by configuring a 'Master Password,' you can limit who has access to your Microsoft Account.

Installing Android Applications on Windows 11

Android apps are programs that run on your smartphone or tablet. Android apps can now be installed and run on the new Windows 11 operating system. You must first install the Android subsystem and then the Amazon store to run them.

To install Android apps on Windows 11, you must first determine whether your system meets the system requirements. The following are the prerequisites for installing Android applications:

- Your system's OS build must be 22000 or higher.

- RAM should be at least 8 gigabytes in size.

- You must be a member of the Windows Insider Program's Beta Channel.

- You will turn on virtualization for your computer. To enable virtualization on your computer, go to the Taskbar's Search icon and select turn on or off Windows features. Simply click on it. Enable the Virtual Machine Platform and Hypervisor options from the menu.

- You must have the most recent version of the Microsoft Store. Go to the Microsoft Store settings and check for updates. Check for the most recent updates.

The only disadvantage is that this works only if your region is set to the United States. If you are not in the United States, you will almost certainly need a VPN to use it. You can, however, change the region of your system. Go to your computer's settings and look for the region. Then, select the United States on the country or region dropdown menu. This should work, but you should use a VPN if it doesn't.

To use the Amazon Appstore, you must have an Amazon account in the United States. A VPN can also be used to accomplish this.

You can download and install Windows Subsystem for Android when your computer meets the requirements. Simply follow the steps outlined below:

1. Open the **Microsoft Store**. On the search box, search for **Amazon Appstore**.

2. Click on it and click **Install**. Then, click **Set Up**.

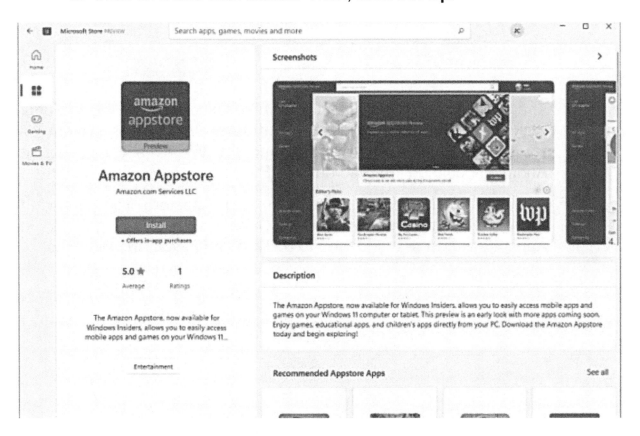

3. You will be asked to download the **Windows Subsystem** for Android on the prompt. Click on **Download**.

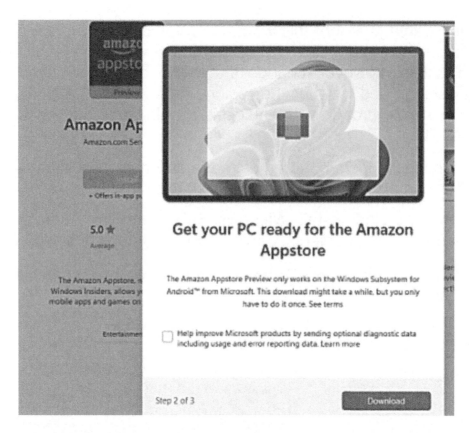

4. The download process will take a while. Once the download is done, click **Next**, then **Restart your Computer**. After your system has restarted, the Amazon Appstore and the Windows Subsystem for Android should be installed on your PC.

5. Now, you will need to set up your Amazon Appstore. You will need to **Sign In** with your Amazon account. Once you are done signing in, the Appstore is now ready for you to browse and install Android apps.

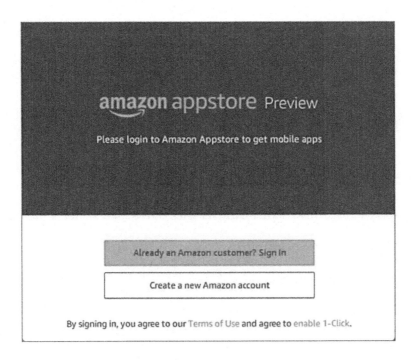

To install an Android app, simply:

1. Go to the **Amazon Appstore.**

2. Search for the App you want to download. Click on the **Get** option to install it on your system.

3. The App will be downloaded and work like other desktop apps on your computer. You can pin your Android apps to the Taskbar or Start menu.

How Do You Clone a Hard Drive to an SSD in Windows 11?

Several cloning applications are available in Windows 11 for converting a hard disk drive (HDD) to a solid-state drive (SSD). Because the steps for each software may vary, the instructions below specify the steps to take for specific software.

Ensure the SSD is connected to your PC via one of the appropriate ports before cloning. Using the cloning application AOMEI Backupper Standard:

1. Get **AOMEI Backupper Standard** and install it.

2. Launch the cloning application that was previously installed.

3. On the left, select **Clone**.

4. Next, from the options on the right, select **Disk Clone**.

5. Select whether you want to clone your operating system and data or just your files.

6. Choose the source disk, which is the HDD to be cloned.

7. Select the SSD as the destination disk.

8. Finally, click **Next**.

9. Next, at the bottom of the screen, check the SSD alignment option, and then click **Start Clone** to begin the process of cloning from HDD to SSD. Be patient until the process is finished.

How to Repair Crashed Software in Windows 11

Many users have complained on the internet about the software crashing on their PCs after installing Windows 11. This issue will be resolved when Microsoft releases the official version by the end of the year. However, for the time being, the methods outlined below can be used to resolve this issue. Another common cause of Windows crashes is an outdated driver. This problem can be resolved quickly by updating the drivers for your devices. Realtek audio drivers frequently cause such issues. You can try updating it to see if that resolves the problem.

1. Click on **Win+R** to launch **Run**.

2. Enter the **Device Manager** and then choose the first result to access the Device Manager.

3. Expand the sound, video, and game controllers.

4. Right-click on **Realtek(R) Audio** and then choose **Uninstall Device**.

5. Tap **Uninstall** from the pop-up interface to complete the process.

6. The driver will then be uninstalled from your computer. After that, you can then restart your computer. Then, the latest driver will be installed automatically on your computer.

How to Change Your Keyboard Layout

To change your keyboard layout, follow these steps:

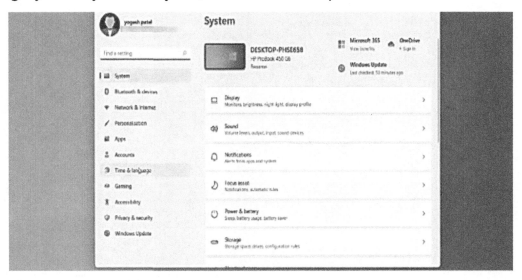

1. Open the **Settings** App.

2. Click on the left side of the screen on **Times and Languages**.

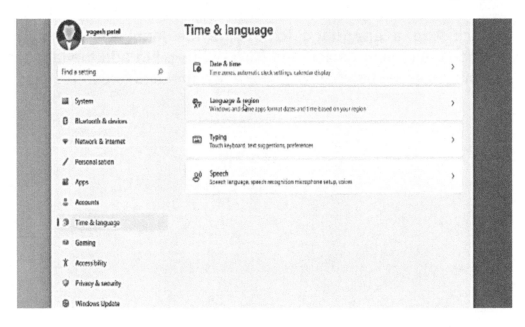

3. Select **Language and Region.**

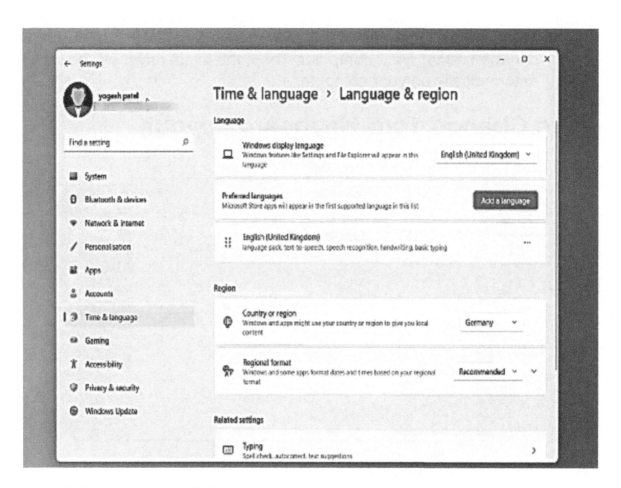

4. You can see all the languages your operating system supports. In this image, English (United Kingdom) is the preferred language.

5. Click **Add a Language** to change the language." Search for the language of your choice and click on Install to add the language. The installation will begin. It will take a few minutes to complete.

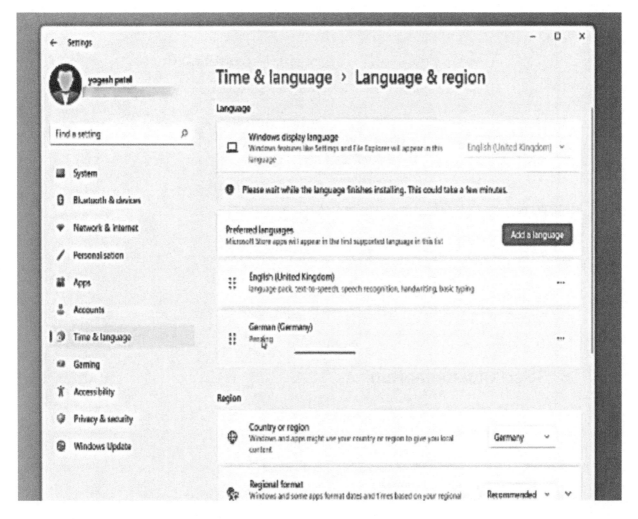

6. You will be need to sign out of Windows when the installation is finished in order for the changes to take effect. Do so by clicking the **Sign Out** button to sign out of Windows, then sign back in again.

7. The new language has been successfully installed; this new keyboard layout is ready to be used.

How to Fix Bluetooth Using Troubleshooter

1. Click on the **Start** button.

2. Locate **Settings**.

3. Select **System** on the left, go down on the right and select **Troubleshoot**.

4. Underneath *troubleshoot,* select *other troubleshooters.*

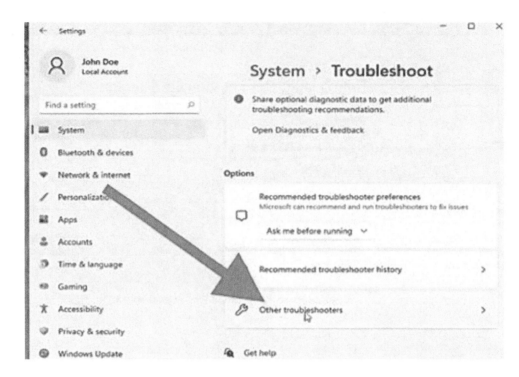

5. Select **Bluetooth>Run**.

How to Screenshot on Windows 11

1. Click on the search icon, type **Snipping Tool,** and click on it.
2. Click **New** at the top of the windows screen.

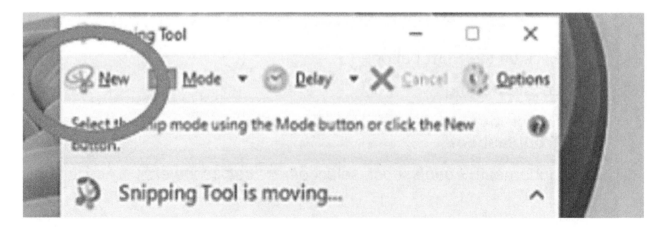

3. You can then select any area you want to take a screenshot of.

4. You can also save the screenshot

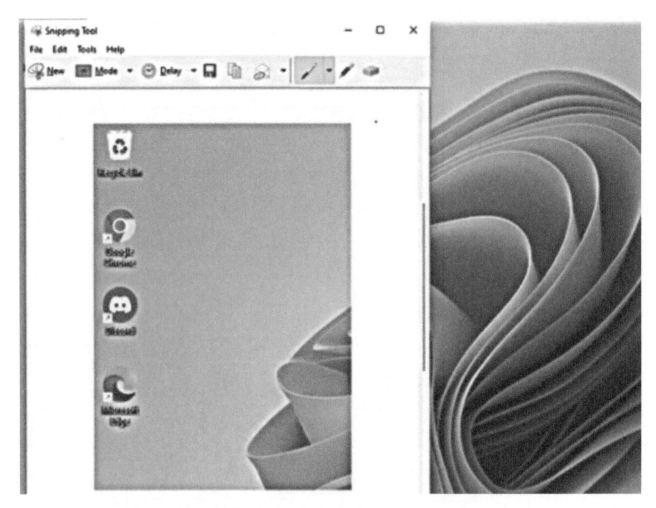

How to Factory Reset on Windows 11

1. Click on **Search,** then type **Settings**.

2.   Click open, scroll down and locate **Updates and Security.**

3.   On that window, go to the **Recovery Tab.**

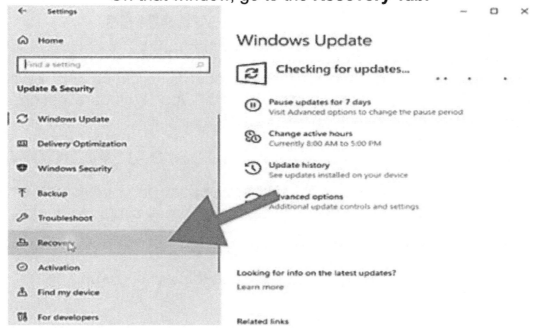

4. Next, click on **Reset PC.**

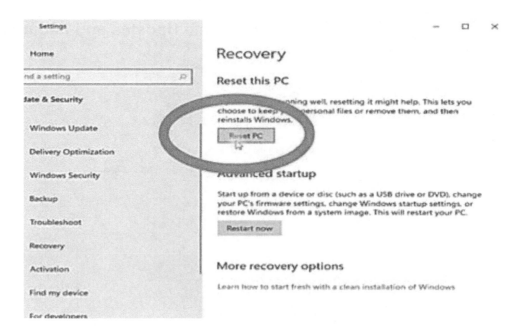

5. It will give you two options; **Keep my Files** or **Remove everything**.

6. Make a choice and go for it. The system will reset accordingly.

How to Switch Between Keyboards

The keyboard layout button will appear on the **Taskbar** once you have added a new keyboard. To switch between keyboards, click on this keyboard layout button by the bottom right, and a list of all your keyboard options will appear from which you can select the one you like.

How to Enable Touch Keyboard in Windows 11

You might want to make your keyboard appear on your screen while your PC runs on a Windows 11 operating system. It is pretty simple to do this.

1. Right-click on the **Taskbar**.

2. Click on **Taskbar Settings**, and this will show up.

3. You will notice a keyboard icon in the right-hand corner of your Taskbar in Windows 11. Enable the **Keyboard Toggle**, and your **On-Screen Keyboard** is ready to be used.

How to Add Shortcuts to the Start Menu

In addition, Windows 11 has enabled a feature in the Start menu that allows you to add shortcuts to File Explorer, Settings, Pictures, Videos, Documents, Videos, Downloads, and other programs in the lower section of the Start Menu.

1. Navigate to **Settings** on your system.

2. *Proceed to* **Personalization** *and then to the* **Start.**

3. Tap on **Folders**.

4. Toggle on the shortcut for any item you want.

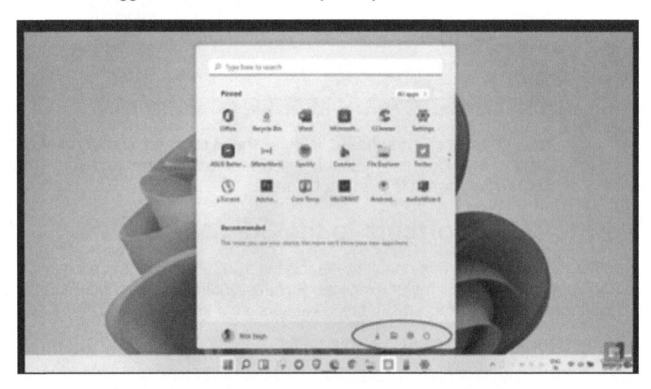

The enabled shortcuts will now be displayed on the right-hand side of the lower section of the start menu, as shown in the pic above.

How to Enable Clipboard History on Windows 11

The Clipboard was introduced in the previous Windows 11 version 1809 and has remained a prominent feature of Windows since then. Naturally, it is not enabled by default, as it is in Android OS; you must go to the Windows settings and manually enable it.

1. To access the Windows settings, simultaneously tap and hold the **Windows** and **I** tabs. After you've opened the settings, go to the **system**, scroll down to the bottom, and select **Clipboard**.

2. To activate the clipboard history, toggle it on/off, and the history will be displayed immediately.

3. After you've enabled the feature, you can use it wherever you want on your PC.

How to Use Different Keyboard Layouts

You can customize the keyboard layouts in Windows 11 during installation. The available layouts can still be modified. This allows you to add or remove them until you find the one that is right for you or speaks another language. You can change the layout's input settings if you need a specific character from another language, such as Portuguese or Spanish.

Regardless of your choice, you can add, remove, and change hardware and touch keyboard layouts in Windows 11.

How to Configure Keyboard Layouts in Windows 11

To add layouts to Windows 11, perform the following steps:

1. Continue by tapping on the **Settings** menu.

2. Select **Time & Language** from the dropdown menu.

3. Select the default language from the **Preferred Languages** section.

4. Select the **Options** tab.

5. Tap the **Add a Keyboard** icon to the right of the **Keyboards** section.

6. Select the keyboard layout you want to use.

7. Steps 5 and 6 should be repeated to add more layouts.

8. Once the steps are completed, the new keyboard layout will be added to the PC. You have the option of switching between different types.

How to Modify the Keyboard Layout in Windows 11

Changing keyboard layouts is a simple process that will reconfigure the keyboard keys on them. The implication is that a new character will appear when you use the keyboard. To switch between different Windows 11 keyboard layouts, you must:

1. Tap the **Input Indicator** button in the bottom-right corner of the **Taskbar**.

2. Choose a different layout.

3. Change the keyboard layout from the Taskbar's Windows.

4. Repeat the first and second steps to return to the keyboard's layout.

5. Once you've finished the steps, you'll be able to type with the new keyboard layout.

How to Remove Keyboard Layout in Windows 11

1. Go to the **Settings** menu and select it.

2. From the dropdown sub-menu, select **Time & Language**.

3. Choose a language.

4. From the **Preferred Languages** section, select the default language.

5. Select the **Options** tab.

6. Select the target keyboard from the **Keyboards** section's list.

7. To remove the item, press the **Remove Button.**

8. Steps 6 and 7 should be repeated to remove any remaining layouts.

9. When you finish the steps, the target layout you selected will be removed from the system.

Emoji Keyboard in Windows 11

The availability of a set of emojis in the emoji keyboard is one of the most significant additions to the user experience on computers today. Windows 11 gives computers a strange mobile feel by incorporating an emoji keyboard, which allows users to chat online and express themselves without having to type how they feel.

We became acquainted with the use of emoji on our Android/iOS phones and tablets over time, and it has since been incorporated into how we express ourselves in the social media space. Windows 11 has evolved over time and now includes a hidden emoji keyboard. Here's how to get to it.

How to Use Windows 11 Emoji Keyboard

The emoji keyboard is visible on any platform your computer screen shows, including the home screen. You can access the emoji keyboard using the appropriate key combinations (Shortcut).

Use the Shortcut (Windows +; full stop) or (Windows +; semi-colon)

To access the emoji keyboard, press the **Windows** key along with the **full stop** key or the **Windows** key along with the **semi-colon** key. By pressing these key combinations, the emoji picker in the bottom right corner of your screen will appear. To insert an emoji into your text, open your text editor and click on the desired character. Unless you close it, the Windows 11 emoji keyboard is always open.

Use the Windows 11 On-screen Keyboard to Access the Emoji Keyboard

To do so, go to the **Start** menu or the **Windows** key button and type **On-screen keyboard.** When the keyboard appears, click on the emoji icon button beside the spacebar. After that, the alphabet will be replaced with emojis, which you can now use.

Windows 11 emoji keyboard is more sophisticated than previous versions of the Windows emoji keyboard. It has a better search option, gifs, more symbols and emoji characters, and a section of frequently used emojis.

How to Access the Command Prompt in Windows 11

On your Windows 11 computer, you can easily launch a command prompt. You can use the Windows Terminal, the Search icon on your Taskbar, or pin a command prompt to your Taskbar for quick access.

A terminal program available to command-line users is Windows Terminal. PowerShell, Command Prompt, and Azure Cloud Shell are all supported. You can open Command Prompt in a new tab or configure the program to open CMD on startup.

To open Command Prompt, simply:

1. Right-click the **Windows Start** menu and select **Windows Terminal** from the context menu. Then, select **YES** to continue.

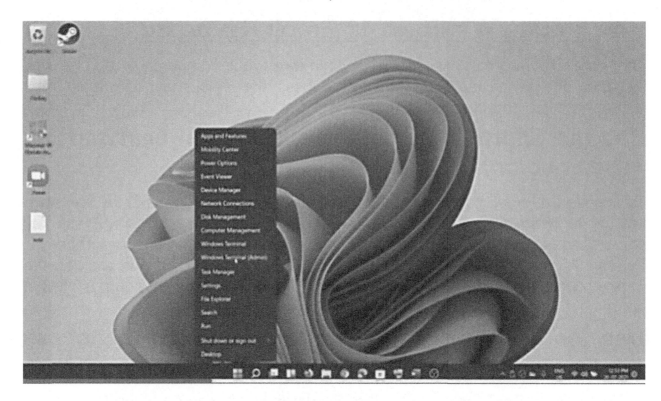

2. Click on the dropdown **Arrow Icon** and select **Command Prompt**. Command Prompt may also be launched by pressing the **keyboard's CTRL + SHIFT + 2 buttons.**

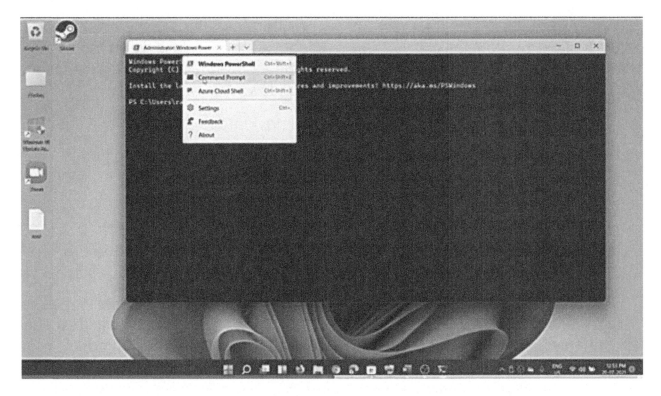

3. A new tab will appear with the CMD window.

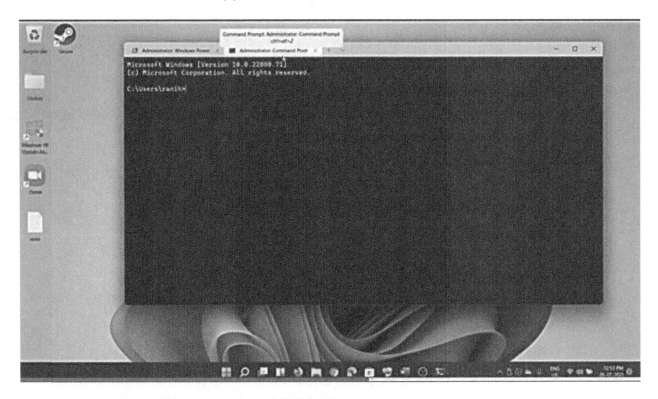

How to Go Back to Windows 10

If you believe you made a mistake by entering the Windows 11 beta, or if you wish you had stayed on Windows 10, you can still do so. When the bugs become too much to handle, most users consider this. This is why downloading beta versions on your official PC is not recommended. While you wait for the official Windows 11 software, which will be released during the holiday season, you can easily downgrade your PC back to Windows 10.

1. To begin, open the **Start** menu and navigate to **Settings**.

2. Click on **Windows Update** at the bottom left of the settings page.

3. Select **Advanced Options**.

4. Scroll down and choose **Recovery**.

5. On the recovery page, click the **Go Back** option next to the previous version of Windows. This will start the installation of Windows 10.

6. When you click the back button, you'll be taken to a page that asks why you want to go back. Choose the option(s) that best describe your experience. You can also use the text field to tell Microsoft why you're returning. This will assist Microsoft in improving its services to serve you better.

7. After providing feedback, click **Next**.

8. You'll see an option to **Check for Updates** on the next page. Because there have been no updates, click **No Thanks**.

9. Click **Next**, then **Next** again.

10. Go back to an earlier build by clicking the button. This will begin the installation of Windows 10.

11. After the restoration process is complete, you must make some changes to your Windows insider account to prevent Windows 11 from installing automatically again. To do so, go to the **Start** menu.

12. Select the **Settings** icon.

13. Click on **Update & Security** on the settings page.

14. At the bottom of the left menu, select **Windows Insider**.

15. Turn on the **Stop Getting Preview Builds** option to prevent Windows from automatically updating to Windows 11.

16. **Restart** your computer.

How to Use the Transparency Effect in Windows 11

The added transparency effect makes your screen slightly transparent when accessing the Settings, Taskbar, and Start menus. To activate the transparency effect in Windows 11, follow these steps:

1. Launch the **Settings** application.

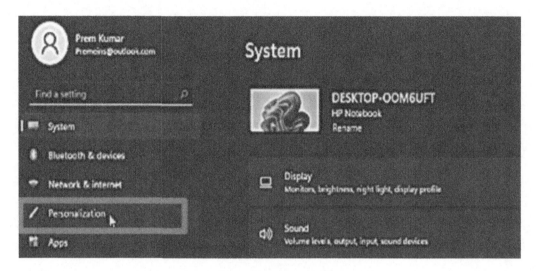

2. On the left-hand side, click **Personalization**.

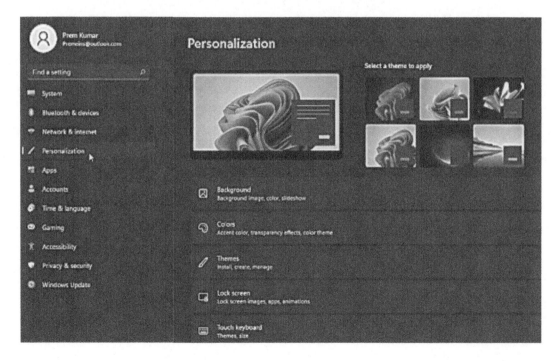

3. Under this, click on **Color**.

4. After you click on **Color**, you will see an option that says **Transparency Effects**, which is only available if you only have Windows 11 installed on your PC. Turn it on and close the **Settings** App.

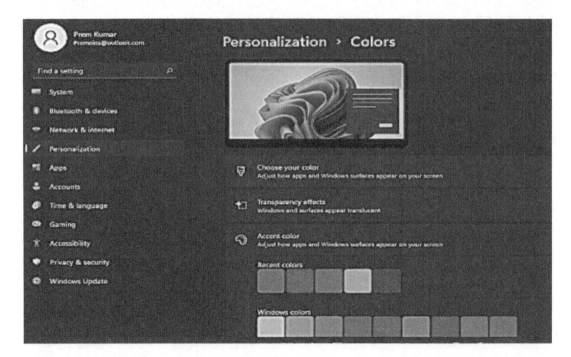

How to Disable Windows 11 Transparency Effects

It is easy to turn off the transparency feature that comes with Windows 11 if you don't want it. To do this, follow these steps:

1. Open the **Settings** App.

2. Click on **Personalization** on the left-hand side.

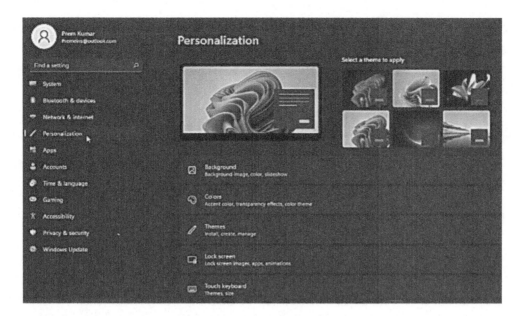

3. Under this, click on **Color**.

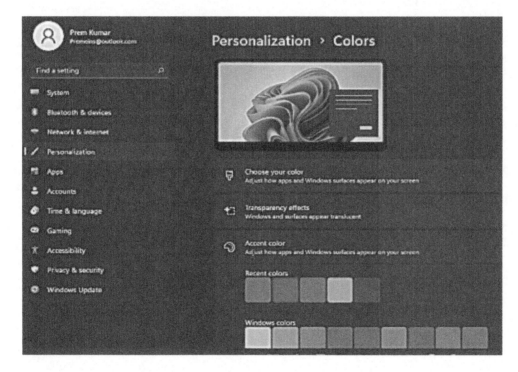

4. After you click on **Color**, you will see an option that says **Transparency Effects**, which is only available if you have Windows 11 installed on your PC. Turn it **Off** to disable transparency and close the **Settings** app.

How to Open Your File Explorer in Windows 11

File Explorer is one of an operating system's most commonly used tools. This is where we keep our belongings and use them for various purposes, such as accessing our files and folders or creating a new folder. There are several ways to launch File Explorer in Windows 11, some of which will be covered here.

Access Your File Explorer from the Taskbar

The File Explorer shortcut is pinned to the Taskbar by default in Windows 11. You can simply click on the icon to open the tool.

Select it from the Start Menu

If you already have File Explorer pinned in your Start Menu, pressing the Windows button to open it will take you to it by clicking on the **Pinned** option. If it isn't pinned, click the **All Apps** button to see a complete list of all the apps available on PC. Scrolling down to the letter **F** will take you to the **File Explorer** app, which is listed alphabetically.

Launch File Explorer by Searching for and Opening It

On the Taskbar, click the **Search** icon. When you search for **File Explorer**, the first result will be your file Explorer app. Just click on it.

Using a Shortcut Keyboard

Press **Windows key + E** on your keyboard to launch File Explorer.

Run Commands to Open Your File Explorer

1. Open the **Run** prompt by pressing the **Windows key + R.**
2. Enter **File Explorer** and press **Enter** or the "OK" button.

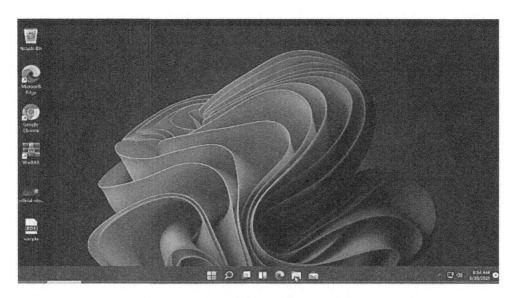

How to Enable Classic Ribbon Menu in File Explorer

With the new Windows 11, there is an updated version of File Explorer in which the classic ribbon menu is absent. However, you can enable the classic ribbon menu back in File Explorer.

1. Open **Start** on Windows 11.

2. Search for **Regedit.**

3. Click the top result to open the Registry Editor.

4. Browse this path on your PC **HKEY_LOCAL_MACHINE\SOFTWARE\Microsoft\Windows\CurrentVersion\Shell Extensions\Blocked**

5. Right-click the **Blocked** key, and a list of options will appear.

6. Select **New** and click on the **String Value** option.

7. Name this newly created value **"{e2bf9676-5f8f-435c-97eb-11607a5bedf7}"** and leave its value data empty to enable the ribbon menu in **File Explorer**.

8. Press **Enter** to save your changes

9. **Restart** your PC. The classic ribbon menu should be enabled by now.

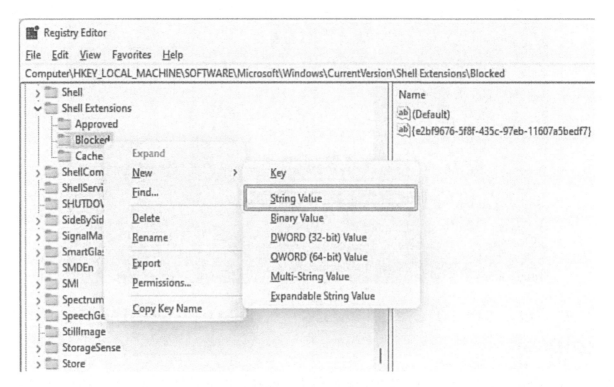

How Do You Change from Standard User to Administrator in Windows 11?

Standard user accounts and administrator accounts are the two types of user accounts in Windows 11. New user accounts in Windows 11 are created as Standard by default, but users can upgrade to Administrator accounts anytime. Standard accounts have fewer options than Administrator accounts. An administrator account, for example, will give you access to all files on the PC, the ability to change other user accounts, install hardware and software, change security settings, and much more.

In contrast to a Standard user account, which restricts your activities, having an Administrator account grants you full access to Windows 11. A Standard User can only use pre-existing applications, cannot install or uninstall software, and cannot delete user accounts. There are several ways to switch from Standard to Administrator in Windows 11.

Navigate to Settings and Select Administrator

1. Launch the **Settings** application.

2. Select **Accounts**.

3. Select **Family and Other Users.**

4. If there is more than one user on the OS, click on the account you want to change from Standard to Administrator.

5. Under that user's account, select **Change Account Type.**

6. Administrator and Standard user options will be made available. To save your changes, click **Administrator** and **Ok**.

Switch to Administrator Mode Using the Control Panel

You can also switch to the Administrator account via the Control Panel.

1. Search **control** in the **Windows Search** bar and select **Control Panel** from the results.

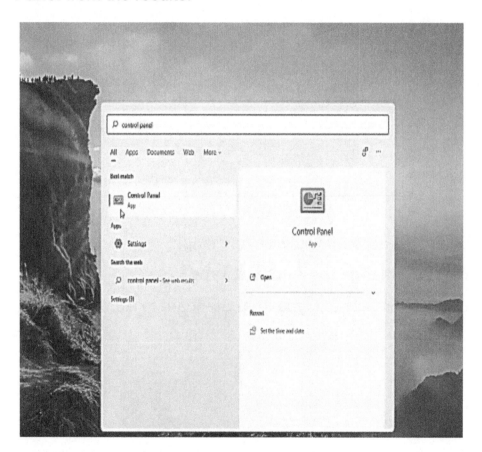

2. Change the **View By** option to Small Icons in the top right corner and click on **User Accounts.**

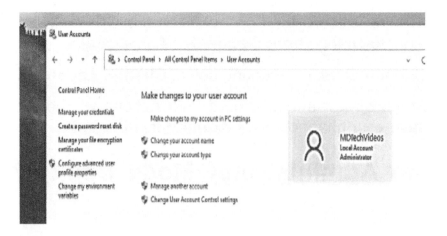

3. Click on **Manage Another Account** from the list of options.

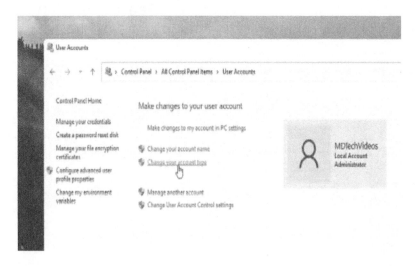

4. Select the account you wish to change.

5. Click on **Change the Account Type**.

6. Change the account type from Standard to Administrator.

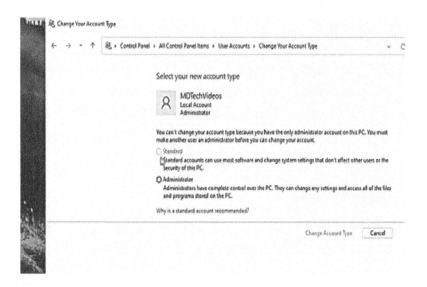

7. Click on the **Change Account Type** button at the bottom to save your changes.

8. You will be automatically returned to the previous screen, showing that the particular account has been changed to the Administrator account.

Change the Administrator Making Use of Command Prompt

1. In the **Windows Search** bar, type **Command Prompt.**

2. On the right, click **Run as Administrator**.

3. Enter **Net User** and press **Enter** to display a list of all the local user accounts on your computer. Make a note of the account name you want to change to Administrator.

4. Enter the command Net Local Group Administrators "name" /add into the command line. The "name" field should contain the name of the local account you want to convert to Standard that you noted earlier.

5. The Standard account has been renamed Administrator.

To revert the Administrator account to Standard, run the command net local group Administrators "name" /delete. The "name" is the name of the Administrator account. Follow the steps above to change it through the control panel or settings, and then select "Standard user" when prompted to "Change account type."

Windows 11's Quick Settings

Microsoft redesigned the Quick Settings panel in Windows 11 with a better UI design and a more usable Quick Settings menu. Quick Settings gives you access to various frequently used functions that vary by device. You can customize this tool by adding or removing functions from the Quick Settings panel. The default functions in the Quick Settings panel are wi-Fi, airplane mode, bluetooth, accessibility, battery saver, focus assist, volume, brightness, and wi-fi.

Adding or Deleting

You must open the Action Center to add or remove a Quick Setting. Click the 'Action Center' icon on the Taskbar or press WINDOWS + A to access it.

1. To add a quick setting, right-click any of them, choose Edit Quick Settings, or click the Edit Quick Settings icon at the bottom.

2. Select the **Add** option at the bottom.

3. There will be a list of all available **Quick Settings**. Select which one you want to add to the **Action Center**. The ones you select will immediately appear in the Action Center.

4. After you've added the required quick setting, scroll down and click **Done** to save your changes.

Removing Quick Settings

1. To remove a quick setting, right-click on any of the tiles again, select **Quick Edit Settings** from the menu, or click the Edit Quick Settings icon at the bottom.

2. Then, click the **Unpin** icon to unpin it in the upper-right corner of any quick setting.

3. After removing the necessary quick setting, scroll down to the bottom and click **Done**.

Note: You can re-add any **Quick Settings** you've removed at any time by selecting them from the list and clicking the **Add** button.

Using Windows 11 to Connect to a Wi-Fi Network

To connect to a wi-fi network via the Taskbar, use the following steps:

1. Click the **Network** icon in the bottom right corner of the Taskbar.

Note: You can also access the wi-fi network by opening **Action Center (Windows key + A)** and tapping the **Network** button in the **Quick Activities** section. If you can't find the button, choose the **Up** arrow button on the left-hand side.

2. If you want to connect, select the **Wireless Network**.

3. Tick or select the **Connect Automatically** checkbox.

4. Choose the **Connect** option.

Note: If no wireless access points are listed, select the wi-fi button to activate the adapter.

5. Check the **Network Security** key, which also acts as your password.

6. Choose the **Next** option.

7. Check to see if the device should be visible to other computer systems on the network.

NB: While using the wi-fi connection, the PC will connect to the network.

Automatic Reconnect

After removing the adapter, Windows 11 allows reconnecting the device automatically. Follow the steps below to configure the wi-fi adapter to reconnect automatically on Windows:

1. In the system tray, click the **Network** icon.

2. Deactivate wireless connectivity by selecting the **Wi-fi** button.

3. Use the following options to select when you want to reconnect automatically:

   - Within an hour
   - Manually
   - Within four hours
   - Within the next 24 hours

As a result, Windows 11 will not attempt to connect to a wireless network until you specify it. If you select this option, your device will automatically connect to your previously linked network.

Installing Fonts on Windows 11

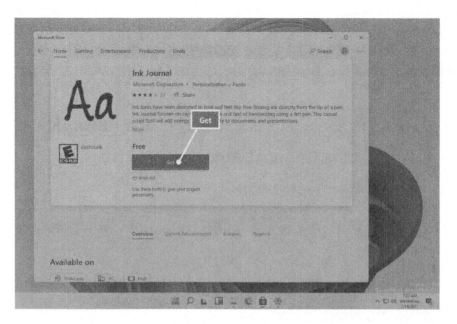

Utilizing the Microsoft Store to Install Fonts

1. Start by going to the **Microsoft Store**. The Microsoft Store offers an enormous choice of paid and free text styles, making it the most helpful option for some clients. To start, go to the store and quest for **Text Styles**.

2. Select a font. Select the ideal text style by tapping on it.

3. Start by clicking **Get**.

4. The picked text style will be introduced naturally close to different text styles previously introduced in Windows 11.

Downloading Fonts Manually

1. Find a reliable source.

2. Download the font pack of your choice.

3. Save the record as a **.zip** or **.rar** augmentation. To open something besides a .zip record, we suggest utilizing pressure programming like **WinRAR or 7Zip.**

4. Uncompress the packed record. Don't stress over the extraction area; ensure the record is saved to a recognizable area, like my reports or the work area.

5. Actuate the font file. Users should see two catches at the upper left of the window whenever it has been opened: **Print** and **Introduce**.

Install your new text style and utilize it.

How to Change the Primary Monitor in Windows 11

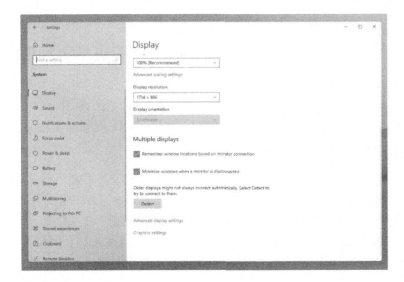

Setting up your display is basic; however, newbies may become confused in the center of Microsoft's most recent makeover of the Windows settings program.

The **Settings** application, which has a supplanted **Control Panel** now, works and has most things in a similar area as the earlier OS, although it might appear somewhat confused.

Whenever you have shown up, setting up a numerous screen work process is basic, and you'll be fully operational in a matter of seconds, including picking which screen to use as your principle show.

How Can I Change the Primary Monitor?

So, you want to change your main monitor in Windows 11, but you don't know how because of the changes in the new OS. Don't worry; these are the only steps you'll need to complete the task and have your combat station operational as you desire.

Fill in Your Preferences or Settings

First, navigate your Settings menu. You can get there by going to the main menu and then selecting settings in the pop-up window.

However, nearby is an inquiry symbol, which allows you to type in **Change Principle Show** to go directly to the appropriate settings page without going through anything else. The search bar trick also eats away at Windows, allowing you to bypass a lot of Microsoft's helpless association in the settings menu.

Display Option

At this point, you must select **Multiple Monitors**. This option will be displayed if the PC cannot locate the screen you want to move to the new primary one.

If you're having trouble with the PC seeing the screen, you'll need to perform some troubleshooting.

- Above all, ensure that you have connected the line to the correct port. Windows will allow you to run two different GPUs simultaneously, such as NVIDIA and Intel.

- Separate the contraption from the motherboard and into the GPU until further notice. Because most GPUs do not have two HDMI connections, you may need to find a location with either a USB-C connection (in the opening implied for VR) or a Display Port connection.

Note: If you still have problems after doing this, try pressing **Windows Key + P**. This will increase the fast screen settings, which may show only each screen in turn. If it doesn't work after a short period, try another link.

- The final significant option is to update your graphics card drivers and the installed graphics card provided with Intel-based motherboards by going to **Device Manager (Search > Device Manager).**

Your computer should be at the top of the list; right-click it and choose **Output for Changes,** then check that the drivers are up to date. If you use NVIDIA, you can do so through the GeForce Experience, whereas AMD has its own program for this.

If you prefer to use **Device Manager**, right-click on the device and choose **Update Driver** from the menu.

The Monitor Menu

Now that you're in the menu, it'll show you at least two screens, each size, and how you'll move your mouse between them. You cannot simply move your presentations and slide the symbols around, but you can achieve your goal:

The main display is being replaced. Click the icon for the screen you want to use as your primary showcase, and from now on, everything will almost always stack on that screen first.

How to Take a Screenshot in Windows 11

If you want to keep a record of the information displayed on your screen or share what you're seeing with friends or on social media, taking a screenshot of your Windows 11 computer screen may be helpful. Depending on what you're trying to accomplish and how you can take a screenshot in Windows 11 in various ways.

How Do I Take a Screenshot in Windows 11?

Snipping Instrument

The Snipping Tool in Windows 11 is a straightforward and useful tool for capturing the entire contents of your screen, a specific open Window, or manually selected isolated portions.

The Snipping Tool can be found in the **Start** menu or by searching for it, and once you've taken a photo, you can save or copy it to your Clipboard.

Even though it has been available since Windows Vista, the Snipping Tool is still functional. However, because Microsoft has already included a replacement for the Snipping Tool, it is impossible to predict when it will be phased out in future Windows 11 operating system upgrades.

Sketch & Snip

This is the Snipping Tool equivalent in Windows 11. Both options are available in Windows 11, but Microsoft claims Snip & Sketch will eventually be the only choice.

It has many of the same features as the Snipping Tool, but it looks better and works well with the Windows 11 notification UI. It is a more refined and well-designed piece of software that performs the same basic functions as its predecessor.

Capturing the entire screen, a specific window, or manually capturing a specific region all have the same options. Your image is immediately copied to the Clipboard, which can be used elsewhere or opened to save or annotate.

It's accessible via the keyboard shortcut **Windows Key + Shift + S,** which isn't the easiest combination of keys to press at once if you've never done it before. You can also access it through the **Start** menu.

This standard Windows feature is not going away anytime soon. This is such an important feature of the operating system that it has its own button on nearly every Windows keyboard. It can also be as simple as pressing the **PrtSc** button on your keyboard to take a screenshot of whatever is currently on your screen.

How to Reset Windows 11 To Factory Settings

Because Windows 11 is a brand-new Microsoft operating system, installation issues may arise, causing you to become stuck on various screens or even have trouble starting up. Additionally, software flaws may exist, allowing malware or viruses to infiltrate your new Windows 11 computer and cause more damage than expected.

Fortunately, there is a way to reinstall Windows 11 for a fresh start and to resolve any issues.

Depending on your needs, Windows 11 provides three methods for resetting your computer, each with varying degrees of comprehensiveness. Here's a quick rundown of what Windows 11 has to offer.

Refresh Your Computer

This is a good option if you have a few minor issues with your Windows installation and want to undo any changes made to key operating system files. It is not intrusive and allows you to save your files on your computer.

Because you'll have to reinstall a lot of software, it's a good idea to back up any important data associated with the software you've installed before performing a refresh, such as game save files or configuration files.

To refresh your Windows 11 installation, go to the **Start** menu and select **Windows Security**. Select **Additional Info** from the **Fresh Start** section of the **Device Performance & Health** page.

After backing up any critical files associated with software that will be removed during this procedure, you should be ready to select **Get Started** on the **Fresh Start** page.

Following that, Windows will walk you through the refresh process. This procedure is expected to take 20 minutes, but it may take longer depending on the configuration of your system and other factors.

When you're finished, you'll have a clean Windows installation free of malware and bad settings. Other options provide a more comprehensive solution for wiping your computer clean in preparation for a new start. While this will remove the vast majority of malware, some files will remain untouched, so there are other options for cleaning your computer and starting over.

Reboot Your Computer

This is similar to refreshing your computer, but it also allows you to delete all data on your computer. This more thorough system wipe will return your Windows installation to its original state.

If you choose this option, you must create a complete backup of your PC's data, preferably on a USB drive. All files, documents, pictures, movies, and other data on your computer will be erased during this procedure. Because your computer will be erased, this is an excellent way to ensure it is thoroughly cleaned.

After backing up any data you want to keep, you can perform a system reset by going to the **Start** menu and selecting **Reset This PC** from the heading.

Then you'll be given the option of resetting your computer while retaining your data or resetting your computer without containing your data. Keeping your data is the more thorough option, as it will delete any potentially dangerous files that may have made their way onto your computer, as well as any trash files that are taking up hard drive space; however, keeping your files may also be beneficial.

If you are concerned about severe malware infection, deleting all data may be the best option; otherwise, it is a matter of personal preference.

Reset the System

Rather than reinstalling your operating system, you can restore it to a previously backed up state using **Windows System Restore**. Simply choose a previously created Restore Point from when your machine ran normally and restore it.

During the process, any software installed after the restore point and any new drivers or operating system upgrades will be removed. Because this only affects the core operating system and program installations, you will not lose any data stored on your machine.

To restore the system, go to the **Recovery Control Panel**, which you can access from the **Start** menu. Open **System Restore** options will appear, allowing you to restore your machine to a previously saved restore point. You can use the **Configure System Restore** option in this menu to manually create a restore point.

While the system restores the process, your computer will reboot. When it does, you will be taken back to the previously saved restore point, removing any changes to your operating system that have occurred since the restore point was created.

This is useful for undoing changes made to your computer by a software installation and resolving issues and oddities caused by anything that changes your basic operating system setup. It restores settings and configurations quickly. When you install new software, restore points are created automatically, but you should also make manual restore points regularly.

Install Everything from the Start

You can wipe everything and start over rather than attempting to restore your operating system to a previous state using one of Microsoft's tools.

A fresh Windows installation is worthwhile now and then if you want to ensure that you're removing any old trash files, undoing any incorrect configuration settings, and removing any malware that has found its way onto your machine.

Back up critical data and documents to an external drive before performing a complete system wipe. Note: Cloud storage allows for this.

We recommend linking your Windows product key to your Microsoft account. This will simplify future installations by allowing you to log in to your Microsoft account. The product key for the version of Windows you are installing will be retrieved by Windows from that location. The **Activation** menu in the **Start** key allows you to link your product key to your Microsoft account.

Following the completion of these steps, Microsoft provides a program for creating Windows installation media, which can be used on either a USB drive or a DVD, depending on your preference.

A new Windows installation from external media provides a clean slate, which erases all data from your selected hard drive. It is the most drastic and time-consuming option, but once completed, you can be confident that any problems caused by an incorrect Windows installation will be entirely resolved.

Windows 10 to Windows 11 Upgrade

Overall, Microsoft made upgrading to Windows 10 surprisingly simple, and as the official launch date approaches, we expect an even smoother version.

Everything was automated the last time, and everything went off without a hitch for everyone. A software rollout of this magnitude is bound to have some issues, but Microsoft should have ironed out the game-changing flaws.

Is the Upgrade from Windows 10 to Windows 11 Free?

At this early stage, no one knows the exact features, but we can speculate and project that, similar to Windows 8 to Windows 10, there will be a free upgrade path to encourage adoption.

When a new operating system is released, maintaining older systems becomes more difficult. Microsoft believes that the more people upgrade to Windows 11, the better.

There are references to the free update on Microsoft's website, but there hasn't been an outright press statement yet, so we don't know if there are any restrictions. Only Microsoft has stated that the free upgrade will be available for at least a year after its release.

The free upgrade, like Windows 10, will be limited in time (albeit for a long time), so take advantage of it as soon as you are ready to update.

Is Windows 11 Suitable for My Computer?

Microsoft, as it has in the past, has released a program to determine whether your PC is capable of running its new operating system, so you'll be ready to go when the new system is released.

How Can You Tell If Your Computer is Ready for Windows 11?

1. Go to this **website** and scroll down to the bottom of the page to find the download option for the PC Health Check App.

2. Click to close the app and save it to a convenient location on your computer, such as your desktop.

3. Double-click the downloaded application to launch **PC Health Checker**.

When you run this application, you'll discover information about your computer and whether it's ready for Windows 11 when the time comes. Many people report that the tool says their computer isn't capable of running Windows 11, but we're confident that this will be resolved soon.

Windows 11 VPN Configuration

Because your information is critical, you should contact your VPN before configuring it in Windows. Once you have this information, you can begin configuring the VPN:

1. Navigate to **Network** and **Internet > Settings.**

2. To access the design menu, select **VPN**.

3. Choose a VPN connection at that point.

4. Select **Windows** in the VPN supplier field.

5. Give your VPN association a name in the Connection box that appears. If your VPN provider requires you to join with a specific name, you must do so to proceed.

6. Put the location your VPN provided you in the **Server Name** or **Address Box**.

7. Without your VPN worker's URL or IP address, it isn't easy to set up a VPN association in Windows 11.

8. Under VPN type, select the method that you are currently working on. Please keep in mind that choosing the incorrect encryption type may cause issues. If the VPN does not work after you configure it, try again, but this time select **Automatic**.

9. Select **Username and Password** and sign in.

10. With everything correctly filled out, check the **Remember my Sign-in Information** box and click **Save** in the bottom right.

11. You will now be returned to the VPN setup page, where your manual configuration will be displayed in the rundown. Select it and press the **Connect** button.

12. The VPN will be established.

Best VPN to Use on Windows 11

Here are some of the best VPNs you can use on your Windows 11 PC:

- NordVPN
- ExpressVPN
- Turbo VPN
- TunnelBear
- CyberGhost
- Surfshark

- Hotspot Shield

Newly Added Shortcuts in Windows 11

As a reminder, below are the newly added shortcut keys:

Action	Shortcut
Opening Action Center	Win + A
Opening Notifications Panel (Notification Center)	Win + N
Opening Widgets Panel	Win + W
Quick Access to Snap Layout	Win + Z
Open Microsoft Teams	Win + C

Conclusion

Thank you for taking the time to read this book. Owning a Windows PC appears to be a luxury with this new update and likely future updates. One of the reasons why Windows users around the world will always love Windows is its ability to create exciting new features while keeping the overall operating system remarkably simple.

Despite its recent release, Windows 11 is unquestionably the future operating system. Microsoft has always given its customers the best possible user experience. They should expect nothing less than a user-friendly operating system from the new Windows 11.

Of course, there will be significant differences between this new operating system and previous ones, and a user guide will help their customers adjust to this new development.

With the release of Windows 11, the differences and improvements are apparent. The goal of this guide is to analyze Windows 11 and paint a clear picture for the user, allowing them to see the upgrade in its totality and follow the steps in using the upgrade.

Most Windows users can now work in a more productive and pleasurable environment. While it satisfied most Windows users, the new Windows 11 was unappealing to others. They were unconcerned about the removal of specific applications and functions and the redesign. Windows 11 helps you focus on what matters by cutting through the clutter.

However, another noteworthy inclusion made up for this omission. Take, for example, the new Microsoft Store, which combines your favorite apps with entertainment. What else is there? Windows 11 is faster, safer, and more familiar to IT professionals. Now is the time to buy a Windows 11 computer!

The reaction was generally positive when Microsoft announced its intention to release Windows 11. However, they were chastised for the minimal requirements on a PC for a user to use this new development. People are looking forward to the official release, however, because there are numerous new features they want to try. Good luck.

Printed in Great Britain
by Amazon

43875911R00051